The Saints
VOL. II

Text
Louis M. Savary

Illustrations
Sheilah Beckett

Cover Illustration
Michael Letwenko

THE REGINA PRESS
New York

Saint Isaac Jogues, you were a man of great faith and heroism. Help me find ways to tell people how much God loves them.

SAINT ISAAC JOGUES

Isaac Jogues was one of eight Jesuits from France who came to America to bring the teachings of Christ to the Indians. Isaac was ordained a priest in 1636, and was soon sent to Canada to do missionary work among the Huron Indians.

The peaceful Hurons were often attacked by the warlike Iroquois tribe. During an attack, Isaac and many of the Hurons were captured, tortured, and beaten. Isaac escaped to New York, and boarded a ship back to France.

He soon returned to the New World to resume his missionary work among the Hurons. On his way, however, he was captured by a Mohawk war party and beheaded in 1646.

All of the eight Jesuit companions were martyred by Indians in the New World.

Saint Joan of Arc, God called you from your simple life as a shepherdess to lead a nation to freedom. Help me to be brave and respond to God's call.

SAINT JOAN OF ARC

Joan of Arc was a shepherdess who lived a quiet life with her simple family. At that time, her homeland France was being overrun by British soldiers.

As Joan prayed for the freedom of her homeland and the safety of the French soldiers, she began hearing God's voice telling her to go and save her country.

At first, she could not believe God could be asking her to wear armor and ride a horse into battle. Yet the voices continued to urge her, so she lead the fearful French soldiers on to victory. Then she herself crowned Charles VII King of France in his palace at Rheims.

When the king was crowned, Joan asked to be allowed to return to her family, but the king refused. In 1431 some of the jealous soldiers turned her over to the enemy who burned her to death.

Saint John the Baptist, you pointed out Jesus to those who came to you. Help me to recognize Jesus in all the ways He comes into my life.

SAINT JOHN THE BAPTIST

John's mother Elizabeth and Our Lady were first cousins, so Jesus and John were second cousins. John, who was six months older than Jesus, lived in a suburb of the Holy City, Jerusalem.

When they were children, Jesus and John probably visited each other and played together. They both grew up learning about the Temple in Jerusalem and the Holy Law.

When they were about thirty years old, John began preaching near the Jordan River, and baptizing those who repented. Jesus was among those who came to be baptized.

John had the special task of recognizing Jesus when He came. John told his own disciples to follow Jesus because Jesus was much more important than he was.

John was later beheaded by King Herod.

June 24

Saint John Baptist de la Salle, you had a special concern to provide good and holy teachers for children. Help me to learn from all who teach me.

SAINT JOHN BAPTIST DE LA SALLE

John Baptist de la Salle was born in 1651, and is the patron saint of teachers. He wanted to help the badly educated poor children in France. So, with a group of others, he began to help out in a school where the teachers gave their services free of charge. John gave away all his money to the needy, and founded an institute of teachers we call the Christian Brothers. Not only did they provide free schools, but John created new kinds of schools called high schools and technical schools where children could learn a trade.

Since John realized that children often needed special help in learning, he began the first training colleges for teachers. In this way, he prepared a large number of teachers to teach children well.

Saint John Neumann, you taught many children to know and love God. Help me to understand my faith and to talk joyfully about God.

SAINT JOHN NEUMANN

Although John Neumann was born in 1811 in Europe, he came to New York to be ordained a priest. His first assignment was to work among the immigrants in Buffalo. Because he knew seven languages fluently, he could speak about God to many people in their native language. He was a hard worker, visited the sick, comforted the needy, and trained teachers.

He was appointed Bishop of Philadelphia in 1852. When he arrived there, he found only two Catholic schools for children. Within eight years, he opened almost a hundred more. Even though he was a bishop, he still would teach class because he loved children.

John helped the church in the United States grow and prosper. He wrote two catechisms, a Bible history, and a handbook for priests.

Saint Joseph, husband of Mary, you were always aware of God's presence. Help me find God in my life, and be with me at the hour of my death.

SAINT JOSEPH

Joseph was a quiet, hardworking carpenter who kept God's commandments. He loved Mary and wanted to marry her. She agreed, but when Joseph saw that Mary was going to have a baby and it was not his, be became very upset.

In a dream, God's angel told Joseph it was all right to marry Mary. The angel explained how the baby was God's own baby, and Joseph was being given the sacred task of protecting and supporting Mary and the baby Jesus.

Joseph listened to his dream, accepted the task, and became the foster-father of Jesus. Joseph loved Jesus very much, and taught him all he knew about carpentry.

We are told that when Joseph died, Jesus and Mary were present and he died a happy death. Saint Joseph is the patron saint of a happy death.

Saint Jude, you were open to the Holy Spirit's loving energy. Help me to trust in God's care and to come to you when things seem hopeless.

SAINT JUDE

Jude, also called Thaddeus, was one of the twelve apostles, and probably a first cousin of Jesus.

He is often pictured with the flame of the Holy Spirit touching his head. God's spirit at Pentecost so filled Jude with the love of God that he wanted to tell all people about that love.

After Jesus' Ascension, Jude traveled as a missionary to Syria and Mesopotamia. Wherever he went, he taught people to be simple, humble, and prayerful. He made many converts, especially among the Jewish people living in those countries. He sent a long letter to his Jewish Christian friends. "We owe God praise and thanksgiving for His endless mercy," he wrote.

Jude is the special patron of the sick, especially those who are hopeless cases.

October 28

*S*aint Patrick, you loved to make people happy by telling wonderful stories about God. Help me to be able to tell others how much God loves us.

SAINT PATRICK

Patrick was born somewhere in Europe, but he developed a special love for the people of Ireland. In those days, the Irish did not know about Jesus and Mary. Patrick wanted to tell them, so the Pope sent Bishop Patrick to Ireland.

Because Patrick was a very likable person, the Irish people welcomed him. They loved stories and song, and they especially loved the stories Patrick told them about Jesus and Mary. He taught the Christian faith in story form. For example, he explained the Holy Trinity by pointing to the shamrock flower which had three leaves yet was one plant.

Patrick traveled through Ireland preaching the Christian religion. The Irish people have always remained faithful to the heritage brought by Patrick. He died about 461.

Saint Paul, you were an apostle of Christ and a missionary to foreign countries. Help my heart to burn with love for Jesus and for all His people.

SAINT PAUL

Before Paul met Jesus, he had been called Saul. He was a short man, full of energy and emotion. He always acted with great intensity and held his beliefs very strongly.

At first he hated Jesus and persecuted Christians. One day, riding on a horse, he was knocked to the ground by what seemed like a lightning bolt.

During the next few days he began to believe in Jesus, was baptized, and his name was changed to Paul. He went from city to city telling everyone that Jesus is Lord.

Wherever Paul went, he started new communities of Christians. He treated each community like a large family that belonged to Jesus. Paul's love for Jesus was like a fire that burned in his heart. In Rome, Paul's enemies put him in prison, where he died about the year 67.

Saint Peter, first among all the apostles, you showed how even a strong person can be weak. Help us ask Jesus for forgiveness whenever we deny the truth.

SAINT PETER

Simon was an expert fisherman. Jesus chose him to lead His apostles when He changed his name and said, "You are Peter and on this rock I will build my Church."

Jesus preached from Peter's fishing boat, and cured Peter's mother-in-law when she was sick. Jesus took Peter with Him wherever He went.

Peter had his weaknesses. When things became difficult, Peter might talk bravely, but he did not always act so. When Jesus was put on trial, Peter did not go into court but stayed out in the yard. When one of the women there asked Peter if he was a follower of Jesus, Peter denied it. He lied to save himself. Immediately, Peter was sorry, and Jesus forgave him.

At Pentecost, God sent the Holy Spirit into Peter, and Peter was never afraid to tell the truth again.

Saint Rose, through prayer and love you developed your true beauty. Help fill my life with the love and beauty that comes from God.

SAINT ROSE OF LIMA

Rose is an American saint. She was born in Lima, Peru less than one hundred years after Columbus discovered America. At baptism, her parents gave her the name Isabel, but people called her Rose because she was very beautiful.

Rose was so afraid her beauty would lead her into evil ways that she cut off her hair, worked until her hands became rough, and wore ugly clothing.

All around her, people were leading evil lives, and she wanted to make up for their sins. She wanted God to know how much she loved Him, so she did penance for the sins of others. She lived in a little hut and slept on the dirt floor.

She became a Dominican nun, and was known for her power of prayer. The people loved her, and to this day they claim her prayers drove away an enemy fleet that was attacking Peru.

Saint Therese, you wanted only to love God, but you helped many people at the same time. Help prayer to be easier when I find it difficult.

SAINT THERESE, THE LITTLE FLOWER

Therese Martin was born in Alencon, France in 1873. From her earliest days, Therese told her father she wanted to belong totally to God. "You are too young to be a religious sister," he said.

Therese then asked the Pope for special permission. He said it would be all right, and so she entered the French Carmelites at the age of 15.

"I just want to love God," she said to the sisters. Therese was a simple girl and wanted to find easy ways to pray. "People are creating wonderful inventions to make things easier," she said. "I would like to invent a prayer elevator to God."

She is often called the Little Flower because she promised, "After I die, I will drop down from heaven a shower of roses." And that is just what she did.

*S*aint Thomas Aquinas, you were both brilliant and holy. Help me with my studies and help me to become a holy person.

SAINT THOMAS AQUINAS

Thomas Aquinas always wanted to be a priest, but his family tried to stop him. About 1245, when Thomas went to live with the Dominicans, his two brothers brought him back and locked him in their castle for almost two years. The Pope himself heard about Thomas and commanded his family not to stand in his way.

Thomas was very wise and also very holy. In Latin, his nickname was *Doctor Angelicus*, which means the teacher who is like an angel.

Thomas wrote the most famous theology books of all time. All priests and seminarians study his books.

Thomas also wrote beautiful poems and music. We still sing some of his songs in Church. When God asked Thomas what reward he wanted, Thomas said, "Lord, I want only You." He died in 1274.

Saint Thomas More, you knew how to praise God and still be happy. Help me to be cheerful throughout life, and to make as little wrong as possible.

SAINT THOMAS MORE

"Praise God and be merry!" was one of Thomas More's favorite sayings. Thomas was a cheerful man, who loved to spend time with his friends.

He raised a large family, and even adopted several children. In a time when girls were kept in the kitchen, he believed girls should be as well educated as boys, and did so with his own daughters.

Thomas wisely realized there were always going to be wicked people in the world and we would frequently have to deal with them. So he wrote to his friends, "Handle everything as gently as you can. And what you cannot put right, you must try to make as little wrong as possible."

Thomas was beheaded in 1535 by King Henry VIII because he would not compromise his Christian beliefs. He is the patron of lawyers.

*S*aint Vincent de Paul, you happily spent your life giving everything you had to God's poor. Help me to realize that God loves me when I give cheerfully.

SAINT VINCENT DE PAUL

Vincent de Paul was a priest who was most remembered for his kindness. He worked to earn money, then gave it all away to the poor. He brought poor people who were sick to his own home and cared for them. He is the patron of charitable societies.

Poor children were always hanging on his coattails. To them, he gave food, clothing, toys, and all the love that was in his heart.

Vincent gathered a group of men and women dedicated to God. The women, who called themselves Sisters of Charity, nursed the sick and cooked meals for them. The men with Vincent, who called themselves Priests of the Mission, collected food and clothes for those who could not work. After his death in 1660, the Vincentians and the Sisters of Charity continued his work.

ALL SAINTS DAY

Besides the saints described in this book, there are hundreds of other saints whose names are listed in the Church's canon of saints, and millions of other saints in heaven whose names are known only to God. That is why we celebrate a day for all the saints.

What does it mean to be a saint? To be proclaimed a saint by the Church has a lot of special requirements. To be a saint in God's eyes—which is more important anyway—is a lot easier. As long as you believe in Jesus and are trying to live a life that is pleasing to God and loving toward others, God says you qualify as a saint, that is, you belong to the Communion of Saints.

You are probably a saint right now. I hope you will remain among the Communion of Saints forever.